DATE DUE

W9-AFG-344

American Lives

Deborah Sampson

Rick Burke

Heinemann Library
Chicago, Illinois

© 2003 Heinemann Library
a division of Reed Elsevier Inc.
Chicago, Illinois

Customer Service 888-454-2279

Visit our website at www.heinemannlibrary.com

Created by the publishing team at
Heinemann Library

Designed by Sarah Figlio
Photo Research by Dawn Friedman
Printed and Bound in the United States by
Lake Book Manufacturing, Inc.

07 06 05 04 03
10 9 8 7 6 5 4 3 2 1

Library of Congress Cataloging-in-Publication Data
Burke, Rick, 1957-
  Deborah Sampson / Rick Burke.
    p. cm. — (American lives)
Summary: A biography of a young woman who,
disguised as a man, served in the army during the American Revolution.
Includes bibliographical references and index.
  ISBN 1-40340-729-0 (Library Binding-hardcover) —
ISBN 1-40343-104-3 (Paperback)
 1. Gannett, Deborah Sampson, 1760-1827—Juvenile literature. 2.
United States—History—Revolution, 1775-1783—Participation,
Female—Juvenile literature. 3. Women soldiers—United
States—Biography—Juvenile literature. 4. Soldiers—United
States—Biography—Juvenile literature. [1. Gannett, Deborah Sampson,
1760-1827. 2. Soldiers. 3. United States—History—Revolution,
1775-1783—Biography. 4. Women—Biography.] I. Title.
  E276.G36 B87 2003
  973.3'092—dc21

                                    2002154417

Acknowledgments
The author and publishers are grateful to the
following for permission to reproduce copyright
material: Title page, p. 11 North Wind Picture
Archives; pp. 4, 13 Collection of the Mercer
Museum of the Bucks County Historical Society;
p. 5 U.S. Army Women's Museum/Fort Lee,
Virginia; p. 6 Burstein Collection/Corbis; pp. 8, 18,
23 Stock Montage, Inc.; pp. 9, 17, 20 Bettmann/
Corbis; pp. 10, 25, 26 The Granger Collection; p.
12 Ted Spiegel/Corbis; p. 14 Collection of the
Spruance Library of the Bucks County Historical
Society; p. 15 Corbis; p. 16 Geoffrey Clements/
Corbis; p. 21 Getty Images; p. 22 The Historical
Society of Pennsylvania; pp. 24, 27, 28 Hulton
Archive/Getty Images; p. 29 Community
Preservation Initiative/Massachusetts Executive
Office of Environmental Affairs

Cover photograph: North Wind Picture Archives

Special thanks to Patrick Halladay for his help in
the preparation of this book.

Every effort has been made to contact copyright
holders of any material reproduced in this book.
Any omissions will be rectified in subsequent
printings if notice is given to the publisher.

Some words are shown in bold, **like this.** You can
find out what they mean by looking in the glossary.

The cover of this book shows a portrait of Deborah
Sampson, a woman soldier in the Revolutionary War.

Contents

Deborah's Secret

Robert Shurtleff and the other men in the squad of American soldiers watched through the trees. They saw the **Tory** guards walk away from a cave. After the guards were gone, Shurtleff and the others quickly entered the cave. They were surprised to find the cave filled with supplies.

The Tories had been stealing food and supplies from nearby farms. The farmers believed that America should be free from the control of Great Britain. The Tories thought that Great Britain should still be in control.

This is the type of rifle and bullets that soldiers fighting in the Revolutionary War used.

4

The American soldiers loaded their bags with food to take back to their camp. But as they were leaving, a group of Tory soldiers rode up on horses and starting shooting at them. Robert ran as fast as could, but he got shot. He felt a bullet hit him in the neck and then in the leg.

The bullets scared Robert, but not because he thought they might kill him. They scared him because he knew when the doctors took out the bullets they would discover his secret. Robert

This statue of Deborah Sampson is located outside a public library in Sharon, Massachusetts.

was really a woman named Deborah Sampson. It was 1782. Deborah was dressed to look like a man so she could fight for the United States in the **Revolutionary War.**

Childhood

Deborah Sampson's parents were Jonathan Sampson and Deborah Bradford. Her parents' **ancestors** sailed to America on the ship called the *Mayflower*. It landed at Plymouth Rock in Plymouth, Massachusetts, in 1620. Jonathan was related to Captain Miles Standish and John Alden, and Deborah was related to William Bradford. Bradford was the second **governor** of the Plymouth **Colony.**

This painting from 1882 shows the *Mayflower* in Plymouth's harbor.

Deborah was born on December 17, 1760, in Plympton, Massachusetts. There were seven other children in the family. Robert Shurtleff, the oldest child, died before Deborah was born. The others were Jonathan, Elisha, Hannah, Ephraim, Nehemiah, and Sylvia.

The Life of Deborah Sampson

1760	1765	1775	1782
Born on December 17 in Plympton, Massachusetts.	*Deborah's grandmother, Bathsheba, died.*	***Revolutionary War** began.*	*Left Middleborough Massachusetts, to join the arm*

Deborah's grandmother was a French woman named Bathsheba Le Broche. Bathsheba would spend hours telling Deborah stories about Joan of Arc. Joan of Arc dressed like a man and led the French army in its war against Great Britain. Her army defeated the British.

Bathsheba also told Deborah that she named Deborah's mother after a woman fighter in the Bible. These stories taught Deborah that women had fought in armies before.

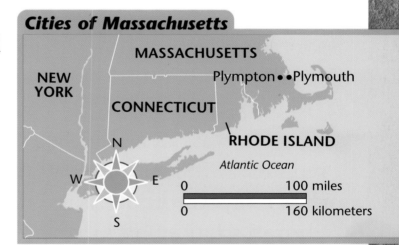

Cities of Massachusetts

MASSACHUSETTS

NEW YORK

Plympton • • Plymouth

CONNECTICUT

RHODE ISLAND

Atlantic Ocean

N W E S

0 — 100 miles
0 — 160 kilometers

This map shows the location of the cities of Plymouth and Plympton.

1782	1783	1785	1827
Deborah is sent to West Point.	*Deborah left the army after it is discovered that she is a woman.*	*Married Benjamin Gannett on April 7.*	*Died at age 66 in Middleborough, Massachusetts.*

Facing Changes

When Deborah was five years old, her life changed forever. Her grandmother, Bathsheba, died. Deborah was very close to her grandmother, and she missed her.

Deborah was expected to help with the work on the farm.

Soon after, Deborah's father left the family farm to become a sailor. He was on a ship headed for London, England. A few months later, Deborah's mother received a message that said Deborah's father had drowned at sea.

Jonathan Sampson

*Some people who study history say that Jonathan did not die at sea. He might have actually moved to Maine, which was part of the Massachusetts **colony,** and started a new family.*

Deborah's mother couldn't take care of all her children by herself. She was able to find homes for her older children. They would live with family members and help on the family farms. Deborah's mother found a job working in the kitchen of another family. She could bring her two youngest children, Nehemiah and Sylvia, with her. But there was no room for Deborah.

This photo shows what a kitchen looked like in Deborah's time. The kitchen is in a building in New York that was built in 1745 and that is now a museum.

Cousin Fuller

Deborah's mother found a home for Deborah when she was five years old. Deborah would live with a family member who the Sampsons called Cousin Fuller. Ruth Fuller was an older woman who never had children of her own. Deborah missed living with her mother, but her life with Cousin Fuller was very good. Cousin Fuller took care of Deborah. She made Deborah dresses and cooked her favorite foods. After three happy years, Deborah's life changed again. Cousin Fuller died.

This drawing shows women making cloth in the 1700s.

In the 1700s, doctors would often see and treat sick people at their houses.

In just three years, all the people she cared about had left Deborah behind. Her father, mother, grandmother, and cousin were no longer with her. Deborah must have felt completely alone.

Deborah's life got even harder when she was eight years old. She was sent to live with Mrs. Peter Thatcher, an 80-year-old **widow.** Mrs. Thatcher was old and sick. Instead of having someone take care of her, Deborah was forced to take care of Mrs. Thatcher. Finally, Mrs. Thatcher went to live with family members. Deborah had to find yet another new home.

The Thomas Family

Deborah was sent to live with Mr. and Mrs. Benjamin Thomas. They had ten boys and lived in Middleborough, Massachusetts. Deborah was a **servant,** but over the years she became more like a member of the family.

Her job was to help Mrs. Thomas cook, clean, wash clothes, and watch the younger boys. She also helped Mr. Thomas with his farm. She was a busy girl who worked hard, but she still found time to do things she liked.

The buildings in Middleborough probably looked a lot like these **colonial** houses in Williamsburg, Virginia.

Deborah probably used this type of **spinning** wheel to make thread or yarn. It was built in about 1800.

Deborah loved to read. She read the books that Mr. Thomas owned. She usually couldn't go to school because she was needed to help around the house and the farm. But she would beg the boys to teach her what they had learned in school each day.

She went hunting with the Thomas boys. She could shoot whatever she aimed at. Deborah became the daughter Mrs. Thomas never had. Mrs. Thomas taught her how to spin **flax** into thread or yarn and sew cloth to make clothes.

On Her Own

Deborah lived with the Thomas family for eight years. She grew tall and strong. In fact, she was taller than the oldest Thomas boy. When Deborah was eighteen, she left the Thomas family, but she stayed in Middleborough.

This schoolhouse was built in Pennsylvania in 1705. It was used as a hospital during the Revolutionary War.

Mr. Thomas helped her find a job as a teacher. Deborah had not been to school that often in her life. But the reading and studying she did in the Thomas family home gave her a good education. Another reason Deborah could be a teacher was that most of the men in the town were away fighting in the **Revolutionary War.**

This painting shows Thomas Jefferson presenting the Declaration to Congress for its approval.

Two years before Deborah moved out, American **colonists** had declared to Great Britain that they wanted to form their own country. In the **Declaration of Independence,** the Second **Continental Congress** told the world that the people of America wanted and needed to **govern** themselves. They were willing to fight and die in order to form a new country. The older Thomas boys went off to fight in the war, and Deborah dreamed of going with them.

The Declaration

Thomas Jefferson wrote the Declaration of Independence in about seventeen days in the city of Philadelphia, Pennsylvania.

Joining the Army

Deborah was the best **spinner** of cloth in Middleborough. After she left her teaching job in the Middleborough school, some women in Middleborough hired her to make cloth and clothes.

While working for a family, Deborah found a suit that belonged to a man who was fighting in the war. Deborah tried on the clothes and was surprised to see how different she looked. Deborah looked like a young man! Deborah had an idea. She would dress as a man and **enlist** in the army.

This painting from 1789 shows what men's clothing looked like in Deborah's time.

One day she put on the suit and walked down the street to sign up to fight for the **Continental Army.** She went into the house of Israel Wood, who was signing up soldiers for the army. Deborah said her name was Timothy Thayer and that she was from the town of Carver, Massachusetts.

This artwork shows the type of clothing that men and women wore in the **colonies.**

As Deborah was signing her name, Israel's mother said, "He holds his pen just like Deborah Sampson." Israel gave Deborah some money for joining the army and told Deborah to show up the next day. The next day, the Woods discovered that it really was Deborah who signed up for the army. They asked her to give back the money.

Trying Again

Deborah was embarrassed by what happened when she **enlisted.** She was sure she wanted to fight for her country, but she wouldn't be able to join the army in Middleborough. She decided that she would try to enlist in a faraway town where nobody knew her. In May 1782, she left Middleborough in the middle of the night. She took with her all the money she had in the world.

To enlist in the army, **colonists** had to go to offices like the one shown above.

Deborah's Adventure

Deborah didn't go directly to Worcester from Middleborough. She had never been far from Middleborough before, so she wanted to see some of the area.

Dressed as a man, in clothes she made herself, Deborah started walking. She walked during the day, and slept in fields or anywhere else she could at night. She was amazed that when she met people on the road they thought she was a young man.

She walked more than 100 miles (161 kilometers) to the town of Worcester. There, she went to the enlistment office. An old soldier squinted over his glasses, asked her a few questions about her weight and height, and quickly let her join the army. She told the man that her name was Robert Shurtleff.

The cities that Deborah traveled to before and after she joined the army are shown on this map.

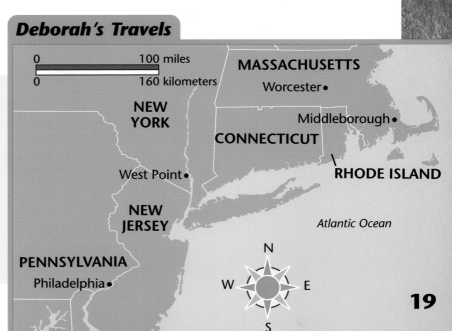

Deborah's Travels

0 — 100 miles
0 — 160 kilometers

MASSACHUSETTS
Worcester•

NEW YORK

Middleborough•

CONNECTICUT

West Point•

RHODE ISLAND

NEW JERSEY

Atlantic Ocean

N
W — E
S

PENNSYLVANIA
Philadelphia•

19

West Point

In May 1782, Deborah was sent with other new soldiers to West Point, an army **fort** in the state of New York. Deborah stayed by herself when she bathed or used the bathroom so the other soldiers wouldn't discover that she was a woman.

When she arrived at West Point, she trained hard to become a good soldier. She **volunteered** for every duty and mission she could. She volunteered for the job to check out the cave where the **Tories** were hiding food. It was there that Deborah was shot.

West Point is shown here in a painting from 1802. The building shown is known as a blockhouse. Soldiers could shoot guns through the openings in the sides of the building.

In this drawing, Deborah is shown in her army uniform.

After Deborah was hurt near the cave, her fellow soldiers lifted her up on a horse and took her back to their camp. She didn't want to be helped by a doctor because her secret would be discovered.

The doctor took care of Deborah's neck, but Deborah didn't tell him about the bullet in her leg. She watched the doctor take out bullets from other soldiers. Then, she went to another tent with a sharp knife and bandages. The third time she tried, she was able to dig the bullet out of her leg.

Philadelphia

Trouble came to the new nation's government when a group of about 300 American soldiers went to Philadelphia. They went there to tell government leaders to pay them money that they were owed. A group of soldiers was sent to Philadelphia in June 1783 to protect the government leaders. Deborah was one of the soldiers.

The money was paid to the soldiers, but people all over the city were becoming ill after catching a fever. Deborah caught the fever, and it made her terribly sick. She was taken to the hospital.

This drawing shows the **Continental Congress** meeting in Philadelphia on September 5, 1774.

Many hospitals were set up during the **Revolutionary War** to help sick and hurt soldiers.

There were a lot of soldiers suffering from the fever. The hospital was overcrowded with sick men who were dying. Deborah was so sick that she was moved to a room on the top floor of the hospital where the sickest men were kept.

One day, a pair of soldiers came to the room to carry off any dead men in the room. They went to Deborah's bed and picked her up to cart her away. She was so sick she could hardly make a sound, but she finally managed to moan. A nurse heard Deborah and had her moved to another room.

Capital City

In 1783, the nation's capital was Philadelphia. It would later move to Washington, D.C.

Surveying Trip

Doctor Barnabas Binney came to check on Deborah. He discovered that she was really a woman in disguise. The doctor told no one about Deborah's secret. He had her moved to his own house so his wife and daughter could take care of Deborah until she was well again. Instead of telling the army about Deborah's secret, he asked her why she had joined the army. She told him of her dream to help her country gain its freedom and to travel to places she had never been before.

Deborah might have been treated in Philadelphia's Pennsylvania Hospital, shown in this drawing. The hospital was built in 1751.

Lightning Strikes

While camping one night on the trip with Colonel Tupper, a bolt of lightning missed hitting Deborah by just inches!

The doctor wanted to help Deborah. He arranged for Deborah to go with Colonel Benjamin Tupper to **survey** the lands west of Virginia. Deborah was one of five soldiers picked to guard the surveyor. But Deborah's fever came back and made her very sick. Colonel Tupper asked an Indian tribe to take care of Deborah until they finished their surveying job. Colonel Tupper's group came back after the job was finished.

Surveyors use instruments called compasses to measure land. George Washington, shown in this drawing, worked as a surveyor as a young man.

Saving Herself

Deborah got better and asked the **chief** if she could go on a hunting trip that some men of the tribe were planning. The chief said she could. Deborah was off on another adventure.

Deborah made an enemy of one old Indian on the trip. He hated Deborah because she was a better hunter than he was. One night as Deborah slept near a campfire, she woke up just as the Indian was raising his tomahawk, or ax, to hit her in the head. Deborah quickly grabbed her rifle and shot the brave before he killed her. The other Indians saw what had happened and told the chief, so Deborah wasn't punished.

This tomahawk was made in the late 1700s.

Deborah returned to West Point with a letter from Dr. Binney explaining that she was really a woman. All of the other soldiers were shocked. Robert Shurtleff, the brave, skillful soldier, was a woman! Deborah left

Deborah is shown here with the letter from Dr. Binney that explained she was a woman.

the army in October 1783 because the army didn't allow women to be soldiers then.

Deborah married Benjamin Gannett, a farmer, on April 7, 1785. They had a boy, Earl, and two girls, Mary and Patience. Deborah also raised the daughter of another woman who had died. When Deborah was older, she traveled around the country and talked to large groups of people about her days as a soldier. At the end of the talk, she would twirl her rifle in a way that a soldier does during a parade. The twirling always got applause.

Remembering Deborah

Deborah Sampson died in 1827 when she was 66 years old. She was able to do well at many things in her life. She was a teacher, even though she did not attend school often. She was the best **spinner** in Middleborough. She was also a good soldier. And at a time when most people in America never traveled far from their homes, Deborah was able to see a large area of the country.

Deborah, seen here in about 1797, is the official heroine of the state of Massachusetts.

This plaque honors Deborah for what she did for the United States. It is in a park in Plympton, Massachusetts.

Deborah was a brave soldier who fought so that the people of America could be free. She fought for what she believed. She showed that women cared about freedom as much as men did. She also showed the country that a woman could be as brave as any man. The United States is the country it is today because of women and men like Deborah Sampson. They cared enough to risk their lives for a land of freedom and opportunity.

Glossary

ancestor member of a family who lived before a current family member did

chief leader of a group of Indians

colony group of people who moved to another land but who are still ruled by the country they moved from. People who live in a colony are called colonists.

Continental Army army of the colonies led by General George Washington

Continental Congress group of men that spoke and acted for the colonies that became the United States. It was formed to deal with complaints about Great Britain.

Declaration of Independence document that said the United States was an independent nation. Independent means not under the control or rule of another person or government.

enlist to volunteer to join the armed forces

flax plant that is used to make strong cloth or yarn

fort building with strong walls and guns to defend against attacks from enemies

governor person who is elected to lead a state. In colonial times, a governor helped lead a colony.

Revolutionary War war from 1775 to 1783 in which the American colonists won freedom from Great Britain

servant attendant or helper

spinner person who uses a wheel that spins to make yarn or thread from flax

survey to measure and make maps of land

Tory colonist who wanted the British to win the Revolutionary War

volunteer to offer or give freely without being forced

widow woman whose husband has died

More Books to Read

Burke, Rick. *Molly Pitcher.* Chicago: Heinemann Library, 2003.

McGovern, Ann. *The Secret Soldier: The Story of Deborah Sampson.* New York: Scholastic, Inc., 1999.

Smolinski, Diane. *Important People of the Revolutionary War.* Chicago: Heinemann Library, 2003.

Places to Visit

United States Military Academy
West Point, New York 10996
Visitor Information: (845) 938-4011

United States Army Women's Museum
2100 Adams Avenue
Building P-5219
Fort Lee, Virginia 23801
Visitor Information: (804) 734-4327

Index